Words or Water

poems by

Li Yun Alvarado

Finishing Line Press
Georgetown, Kentucky

Words or Water

ACKNOWLEDGMENTS
Grateful acknowledgment to the editors of the following journals, in which the
following poems appeared, some in different form or under separate title:

"In Search of Oceans" in *Kweli Journal;* "Something Sweeter than Fish" and "Santa
Barabara de San Cristóbal" in *Centro: Letras;* "Confessions" in *Chicana/Latina
Studies: the Journal of MALCS;* "On Sundays" in *ONSQU Blog;* "His Thumb on
My Belly" in *Dismantle: An Anthology of Writing from the VONA / Voices Writing
Workshop;* "Intercessions" in *New Madrid;* "The Color of Pride" in *de Salinas al
Mundo;* "All I want is a lemon" in *CURA: A Literary Magazine of Art and Action;*
"Aquí" in *PALABRA, A Magazine of Chicano and Latino Literary Art* and *Redux: A
Literary Journal;* "Here" in *Redux: A Literary Journal*

My deepest gratitude goes to my cousin Daniela Alvarado for her gorgeous cover
art. Special thanks to my large, loving, and supportive family, especially Michael
A. Core, Lilliana Santiago, Cornelio Jun Alvarado, Jason Alvarado, Elizabeth
Mendoza, Jared Alvarado, and Dominic Alvarado. I am also grateful for the
encouragement of my friends—the family I found along the way—and my writing
communities: VONA, Acentos, Fordham's Creative Writing Department, Astra
Greece, ¡Capicu!, AROHO, Kweli Journal, and Women Who Submit.

Publisher: Leah Maines
Editor: Christen Kincaid
Cover Art: Daniela Alvarado, photo by Herminio Rodriguez,
                              www.herminiorodriguez.com
Author Photo: Diana Delatorre
Cover Design: Elizabeth Maines

Printed in the USA on acid-free paper.
Order online: www.finishinglinepress.com
                 also available on amazon.com

Author inquiries and mail orders:
Finishing Line Press
P. O. Box 1626
Georgetown, Kentucky 40324
U. S. A.

Table of Contents

For my family:
the one into which I was born
and the one I found along the way.

Para mi familia—en la cual nací,
y la otra que encontré por el camino.

El mar partió mi nombre
en dos

—Julia de Burgos

If Life Began

in the blackness of blue,
then call her: Mami.

We burst from her womb,
groundswell of eternities,

crawled away like crabs
fleshy and raw

beneath homes anchored
to hearts and backs.

We journeyed up mountains,
through deserts, but still,

beneath our flesh,
this ache, it echoes—

Mami. Mami. Mami.

In Search of Oceans

We who are born of the ocean can never seek solace
in rivers: their flowing runs on like our longing.
—Kamau Brathwaite

Lover. Remember when we got high by the Hudson? How I hiked up my baby blue mini skirt and straddled your thighs, your *Sak pasé* rubbing against my *Mi amor*? We were babies then. Running away from Mamas who fed us each night. Reaching for our beloved oceans. Our groping. Our shared ache.

On the phone, you whispered machete revolutions. I disagreed with so much. Thought Dominicanos were Dominicanos. That Dominicano was different from Black. And it was. But it wasn't. But I didn't know about Trujillo then. Didn't know my perejil could make you sweat, could kill. I asked if you could ever love the Spain-white in me. You did not say a word.

On trips to mi islita, I savored deep fried empanadillas full of carrucho, dripping red with garlic-infused sauce, and a warm grease-soaked piece of pan sobao pulled from the belly of el lechón. Mango straddled with strife clung sweet to my lips and tongue. I missed you during those trips to my parents' homeland—my other home—but not that much.

On stolen nights, you wrapped yourself around me. I nuzzled myself into your warmth. Studied your fingers laced in mine. I loved your fingers. Loved how they laced. Loved that something like love didn't always need words or water.

Something Sweeter than Fish

The sadness of migration
is when you realize you've finally spent
more years in your adopted country
than you've lived in your own...
—Roger Bonair-Agard

Mami searches her dreams
for fish. A hint of saltwater
beyond concrete landscapes.

She finds twenty-nine years
of Atlantic currents
pulling her
south.

The news comes too quick:
my brother and I
are like the last to arrive

at the supermarket before
a hurricane, rushing,
only to find sardines and teabags,
no water.

I scavenge for lost
pockets of me.
Find pictures

of her holding us
when she was
younger than we
are now.

In my house,
I make room
for the framed

Yale credential,
bragging rights
that should hang
on *her* walls.

Poems and diplomas:
these are the grandchildren
I have given my mother.

Mami searches her dreams
and sees la vieja y el viejo
(still alive!) still waiting
for their babies' return.

Mami searches her dreams
for fruit. For something sweeter
than fish to take her to her latter years.

The boats
en la Marina de Salinas
assure her,
Your children will be OK.

So she floats
on her back
and she goes.

Fault Lines

We dive into thick masa.
Knead between breaths.
Lace legs. Tumble. Tremble.

You sing hot, loud, liquid
as lava. I sink deep between
colliding fault lines.

Hairs trapped (tongues
pits, fingertips), we giggle
like schoolgirls swapping

secrets until you return
to your husband. Hold out
our love like an offering.

I return to my queen
bed. Reach for myself.
Rock me to sleep.

Confessions

What do you think about abortion?
I wonder if Mami thinks this is about me,

an amusing idea (I have not had sex
in months). *I almost had one,*

she answers. I do not look
at her. I might not have been

here to look at her. But, no,
this is not about me. She

is talking about my sister.
Tu abuela said she would raise

the baby until we could afford you
both. When she was born, they

could not send her away, not even
a year, like they had with me. Instead,

my parents government-cheesed
our lives into normalcy. Only sent us

to la isla during summers. One visit
I teased abuela, *Un día escribiré*

el cuento de tu vida. She laughed
then started her whispered confession.

The husband. The one before Abuelo.
The first child. Then (almost) another.

The back-room. The blood. The sister
who cared for her. *Does Mami know*

this story? Maybe it wasn't just
abuela's Catholicism that gave me

my little sister. I think
about how abortion skipped

a generation. But this
is not about me. I cradle

these confessions. Give
my sister the money.

Plan B

You drove away
before the blizzard.

You speed when you drive.
Anticipate lights turning red
to green, then accelerate.

If that happened
you kissed,
it would be divine
intervention.

In your car, I wear my seatbelt
and hold my breath. *Don't*
take Plan B, you said. But

you didn't say

I walk into the storm.

we are poets each
of us travelers between
history and hope

—Suheir Hammad

On Sundays,

pillows piled high, hand
mirror in left palm, she
leans back, gazes into her

reflection; tweezers tight
between right forefinger
and thumb, she plucks

away a week's worth.

Annual Fast

Dulcinea never launched
a thousand ships. Why
should I? Sometimes
I remember it's a luxury
to whine about the love
question. On Ash Wednesdays,
I fast. Sancho Panza smiles
at me from a vintage Don Q.
I ignore him
                  until Easter.

And his ride was always the roller coaster
for Juanito Xtravaganza

Vogueing drag queen divas,
banjee boys, Madonna,
Larry Levan, our black Buddha,

los negros santeros
dancing all around me:
1986, Paradise in a Garage.

He saw me and thought:
incredibly beautiful boy.
Man of my dreams.
He should look at *me*.

And I was like,
"*Okay*, Keith Haring,
whatever..."

But he was cute
(in a Woody Allen
sort of way).

I was the Puerto Rican
chameleon every place
we went: Morocco, Japan,
Brazil and back.

Then as soon as we landed,
the limo to Coney Island
(he liked the boys there).

And his ride was always
the roller coaster.

I didn't always want
around the world,
off a plane, on a coaster.

But I'd get on
trying to figure out
when the next drop
was coming. The next

drop...

Traveling all over, enchulao,
wedding bands in Japan,
smoking pot at the Whitney,
letting them know:

"we don't have to *look*
like you to *live*
like you."

but the best part was always
coming home: built it, painted it,
cleaned it, cooked it, stretched out

his canvases, helped him
paint. *You know that mural
in Paris?*

And as soon as we landed,
the limo to Coney Island
(he liked the boys there).

Almost none of his friends
from New York were invited
to the funeral in Kutztown.

Later, people saying
these lowlife Puerto Rican
hustler kids brought Haring down.

But we were inspiration,
collaboration,
as he continued
the line.

He did always want
what he couldn't have,
or be. His ride was always
the roller coaster.

Those last three days
he called me
to his side.

I felt he'd finally realized,
if anyone *loved* him
for who he was,

but he knew
he was gonna be leaving
me hanging…

And as soon as we landed,
that limo to Coney Island
(he liked the boys there).

And his ride was always,
always the roller coaster.

Note
The text for this poem is drawn from: *Queer Latino Testimonio, Keith Haring, and Juanito Xtravaganza: Hard Tails*, by Arnaldo Cruz-Malavé.

His Thumb on My Belly

To the right of my belly-
button: purple-black

oval print on sun-kissed
flesh. A spirit pinching

while I sleep. Is it
him? A hint? *Here,*

he whispers. Singed
meat. His thumb on my

belly. *Now you know.*
And they (some strange,

foreign they) say there's
comfort in the knowing.

Basements are forgotten
places where moldy lies

cling to dank walls.
On my back: the prickle

sting of inked flesh.
It knows how to burn.

Bruise. Heal. His thumb
on my belly. My aunt

lights candles, piles
pennies in corners, tells

tales of muertitos who
pinch at night. His

thumb on my belly. His
boys cloaked in black

masks. Friendship?
Folly? When they

faced him, (my thumb
on his belly), not flesh,

not lead, not prayer
could stop the blood.

Santa Barbara de San Cristóbal
San Juan, Puerto Rico

Over two centuries
encase the city:
walls, castles, forts.

El Morro y San Cristóbal
tried and tested four times.
The English: Drake, Clifford,
and Abercromby. Then the Dutch.

May 12, 1898: The fifth test.
Santa Barbara, patron saint
of artillerymen, yells

¡Fuera!

long before *Old Navy-*
inspired *Out Navy!*
tee-shirts turn fashionable
on New York streets.

Strong against a bombing
worse than the lightning
that consumed her

murderous father, she
survives, white stone face
miraculously intact.

May 12, 2008: La bandera
Puertorriqueña wrestles
between La Cruz de Borgoña
and Old Glory while kids

wearing Abercrombie
and Fitch look over
century-old stone walls
at a bay of U.S. Navy ships.

Adiós

Porque la piedra
en esta mano pesa más
que lo que aguanta
tu corazón.

Yo busco placeres
de otros tamaños:

grandes como la culminación
de todos mis pecados
perdonados;

eternos como el recuerdo
y el sabor húmedo
de nuestro perdido San Juan.

Recuerda… *from the Spanish recordar*
which is at root not remember or re-mind,

but pass back through the heart—

—María Meléndez

Intercessions

On his 80th birthday, we celebrate our good genes and his will to fight. The doctors call this remission. Some cancers kill slowly. Give time for poisons and potions to work. Stage four lymphoma is not that kind of cancer. In his case, the doctors said three months. She denied the existence of cancer. Observed the world of medicine and her children's broken English intercessions without a word. The properties of belief and prayer cannot be charted along the periodic table, but, like gravity, their effects can be felt. She worked elements of the other plane. I do not know the details. Only this. He lived. Then kept living. Ten years cancer free. He could not return the favor. When she died too fast for intervention, he sought an old forgiveness that our embraces could not grant. In the end, was that his secret? Papa, when we all thought we would lose you at seventy, did both your women intercede on your behalf?

The Color of Pride
for Jason

I. Puerto Rican Day Parade, Age 5

Your teeth flash bright
as the single white star
on our flag. Inherited pride,
permanent as the flamboyant-
shaped lunar tattooed red
on your chest since birth.

II. Night Crawler of New York City

You discard the waste
of a city with nothing
but excess. Stop

traffic for blocks.
Still, invisibility:
your uniform.

Through black
plastic stench,
others do not

perceive: you
carry your pride
in your pocket.

III. PVT Alvarado

The call of Mr. Softee
signals the eve of your return.
My long winter:
books, letters, keeping house.
Your long winter:
push ups, letters, rifles, runs.

Prickles of red will barely peek
through your scalp like blood-
stained tips of grass breaking
through dried earth.

You will wear new dress blues.
I will wear red. Like your hair.
Like the knot in my chest.
Like the color of the money
that has brought us to this.

All I want is a lemon

plucked from the folds of my skirt,
perfumed with citrus and sweat.

Behind me, las cabras and my cousins
calling baaaa-baaaa-baaaa.

In front, foggy glass pitcher
of sugar water in her hands.

I want to steal a lemon, feel
the sting of spring on pursed lips.

Want to see her, squeezing
fruit again. Her, filling

the pitcher. Her, filling
each of our glasses to the brim.

Aquí

En esta vida falta   espacio
para tanto amar.

Chillidos, murmullos,
acero contra acero,

estos latidos, el tren.
Y soñar es vivir

y dormir es soñar
y aquí, aquí mi niño,

dum   dum   dum

este corazón.

Here

This life lacks   space
for so much love.

Screeches, whispers,
steel against steel,

these heartbeats, the train.
And to dream is to live

and to sleep is to dream
and here, here, my child,

thump thump thump

this heart.

Li **Yun Alvarado** is a Nuyorican poet, writer, scholar and educator. Her work has appeared in several journals and anthologies including: *Wise Latinas: Writers on Higher Education; The Acentos Review; CURA: A Literary Magazine of Art and Action; Dismantle: An Anthology of Writing from the VONA/Voices Writing Workshop; PALABRA, A Magazine of Chicano and Latino Literary Art; Coiled Serpent: Poets Arising from the Cultural Quakes & Shifts in Los Angeles;* and *Modern Haiku.* Her work received an honorable mention for *The Andrés Montoya Poetry Prize* in 2012, and it was selected as a finalist for the same prize in 2009. She is currently the Senior Poetry Editor for *Kweli Journal* and is an alumna of VONA/Voices Writing Workshop, AROHO, the Acentos Fellowship, and Astra Writing in Greece. She holds a BA in Spanish and sociology from Yale University and an MA and PhD in English from Fordham University. She teaches English at Long Beach City College and has had the pleasure of teaching literature, composition, and creative writing—in English and in Spanish—to middle school, high school, and college students in New Haven, Boston, New York City, Long Beach, and the Dominican Republic. Li Yun is a native New Yorker living with her husband in Long Beach, California who takes frequent trips to Salinas, Puerto Rico to visit la familia.